VINCENZO CARRARA is a top executive with experience in Research and Development, Finance, Marketing and Business Operation who worked in different regions and multinational firms. He is the author of several books and the owner of the boutique watch company *Todd & Marlon*. Vincenzo writes about business, self-improvement, fiction and stories for children.

THE TIME RIDER

FIND YOUR DYNAMIC EQUILIBRIUM
IN BUSINESS AND PERSONAL LIFE

VINCENZO CARRARA

Copyright © 2018 Vincenzo Carrara
All rights reserved.
Paperback ISBN: 1985259591
Paperback ISBN-13: 978-1985259591

CONTENT

*"What really decides consumers to buy or not to buy is the **content** of your advertising, not its form."* - David Ogilvy

Why this Book	- 3 -
Live Life to the Fullest	- 11 -
The NEAT Day	- 21 -
100 Time Management	- 27 -
Just Say NO - Save TIME	- 47 -
Delegate Meaning and Techniques	- 55 -
Panic and Procrastination	- 67 -
10 Activities for Commute Time	- 73 -
10 Reasons to Wear a Wristwatch	- 81 -
CLUB 24 - 24 hour watch enthusiasts	- 89 -

INTRODUCTION

Why this Book

"Live in the moment, day by day, and don't stress about the future. People are so caught up in looking into the future, that they kind of lose what's in front of them." – Jenna Ushkowitz

VINCENZO CARRARA

Why this Book

I grew up in a family where time management was essential, and it was always part of the discussions in our daily life. The motto was "hurry up because it is late". It was seldom late though. I'm not sure why, but my family has been always stressed by the concept of time. No matter whether we were going to school, preparing for a trip, going out for pizza or just for food shopping, it was always late... but late for what? The butcher was not waiting for us and the pizzeria was not closing till late. I was missing something, maybe the famous big picture.

So, I grew up thinking it was always late. I thought that maybe over time I was going to be more patient hence less stressed about time. It did not happen! Actually, the opposite. Age got me even more stressed. The older I get the less time I have, which means the less things I can do before leaving. There is no way to stop the time and it gets even worse. The world keeps turning as it did before, but the pace of change of everything is accelerating and I need to keep pace or catchup with it.

It is not only a matter of professional need. My personal life is also driven by the stress of time. I need to put more and more things in this life that is going at a faster pace every single day. Hence a certain day a question came to my mind. Should we enjoy the moment, or shall we do everything faster so to fill our life with the maximum number of experiences?

I did ask to quite few friends and they were split. Some believe that we should enjoy the moment (carpe diem) and make the most out of it without thinking about what's next. They tend to be the most spontaneous and generally they are the ones who don't plan for the long term. Others, on the other end of the spectrum, think that life is short, so we need to maximize the number of experiences we make. They tend to plan well ahead, and they always have something to do. One of those friends plans every weekend of the entire year with specific activities / experience so to make sure they happen. Another, wiser, pointed out that there are certain things we **HAVE TO** do fast and other things we should **ENJOY** doing and to which we should dedicate quality time. Probably this is the answer I was looking for. Hence the key resides on the (personal) definition of what is an "have to" as opposed to what is an "enjoy" activity. I will expand this concept a bit more in detail in the first chapter of the book, but it might of your interest also exploring the chapters about the NEAT day and the 10 things to do during commute time.

But is it really so easy? Not necessarily. Because we are moving and our priorities change. Hence the definition of what is important varies over time. Everything is moving. Our life develops and while we grow up we enter different life stages. When we are kids, then teenagers, then workers (employees or entrepreneurs), maybe parents and grandparents … things are different. We are influenced by diverse factors and we give relevance and meaning to different things. As such, the way we associate priorities and decide how to allocate time might change. But, also the world around us change. When I was a kid I did not have access to mobile phones and PCs for example. Those technologies are changing the way we operate, they tend to reduce complexity and the time required to do things – though sometimes they create new time consuming aleatory needs. By the Moore law those developments keep accelerating and so the impact on our lives. Hence even within the same life stage we might need to revise priorities and time allocation. This is the reason why we need to find our **dynamic equilibrium**. We need to **ride the time**! Every time we and/or the world move we need to identify a new equilibrium.

I've been through lots of personal and professional experiences and some have enriched me on the specific concept of time management. Some were very structured learning, other were only thoughts and considerations made post factum. I'm an engineer so I decided to put some order on those learning and jotted them down. There are different ideas and time management concepts I explored. I tried to divide them in independent chapters – opposite to the structure of the usual books in which every chapter is linked to the previous one. The purpose is to help myself first and you, now through this book, identifying the best method to discover the dynamic equilibrium. I still re-read some of those chapters when I feel lost with the change and I need to find the new equilibrium. This is an ever-green guide for this purpose, especially the chapter on the 100 tips and techniques for time management as well as the other chapter about "say NO', procrastination and delegation.

I'm also passionate about watches (own a small boutique watchmaking company) hence it came natural to me to look at the link between watches and time management. Those ideas are explored in the last two chapters of this book.

The book is written in a very simple language and despite I tried to be direct to the point I might have done some repetition. Those are often done on purpose. In fact, I believe that for this topic the more we repeat the better it is. We tend to read a forget most of the things that relate to work-life balance and time management. Hence to ensure we engrain those concepts I referred to the advice of our Latin's friends who used to say "repetita iuvant"!

You might now wonder whether this will help you. It definitely helped me. Most of my friend wonder how I can achieve so much so fast. I'm an employee, I have my own company (Todd & Marlon LLC), I'm an author of several books, I have a family and lots of hobbies. You want to know the secret? Just read this book.

VINCENZO CARRARA

CHAPTER I

Live Life to the Fullest

"Happiness is a choice. You can choose to be happy. There's going to be stress in life, but it's your choice whether you let it affect you or not." - Valerie Bertinelli

VINCENZO CARRARA

Live Life to the Fullest

Some people want to "live life to the fullest" and few of those seek information about the best way of doing it. For those people there are tons of articles, blogs, websites and books about this topic. It is very easy to get lost in the sea of information and even single articles can be daunting with long lists of tips and tricks. But what is the #1 thing that we should do to really live life to the fullest?

In order to solve a problem, the first thing to do is to define the problem... as simple as that. So why people are not living life to the fullest? This is the first question, the starting point and the number one secret!

Most of the time, people don't live life to the fullest because they are not investing their time in the most important things first! and "first" is actually a key word. Many of us heard the story of the big rocks from Stephen Covey (First Thing First – worth reading!) or similar versions from other people. If this is new to you then worth going through the following paragraph first:

[The lecturer said, "Okay, it's time for a quiz." Reaching under the table, he pulled out a wide mouthed gallon jar and set it on the table next to a platter covered with fist sized rocks. "How many of these rocks do you think we can get in the jar?" he asked the audience.

After the students made their guesses, the seminar leader said, "Okay, let's find out." He put one rock in the jar, then another, then another-until no more rocks would fit. Then he asked, "Is the jar full?"

Everybody could see that not one more of the rocks would fit, so they said, "Yes."

"Not so fast," he cautioned. From under the table he lifted out a bucket of gravel, dumped it in the jar, and shook it. The gravel slid into all the little spaces left by the big rocks. Grinning, the seminar leader asked once more, "Is the jar full?"

A little wiser by now, the students responded, "Probably not."

"Good," the teacher said. Then he reached under the table to bring up a bucket of sand. He started dumping the sand in the jar. While the students watched, the sand filled in the little spaces left by the rocks and

gravel. Once more he looked at the class and said, "Now, is the jar full?"

"No," everyone shouted back.

"Good!" said the seminar leader, who then grabbed a pitcher of water and began to pour it into the jar. He got something like a quart of water into that jar before he said, "Ladies and gentlemen, the jar is now full. Can anybody tell me the lesson you can learn from this? What's my point?"

An eager participant spoke up: "Well, there are gaps in your schedule. And if you really work at it, you can always fit more into your life."

"No," the leader said. "That's not the point. The point is this: if I hadn't put those big rocks in first, I would never have gotten them in."]

In other words, our time is limited and if we don't invest on the most important things first then we would not be able to dedicate quality time hence to live life to the fullest. Assuming you already know what are the "big" things for you in that moment, then the question become - how do we ensure we invest on the most important things first?

Simple - assess your day! Have you ever tried to plot your typical day on a 24-hour map? Depending on the job, or whether one works or not, the typical day might look different. Doing the exercise of mapping activities on a 24-hour map is mind opening!

Every person live life his own way and he/she uses the daily 24 hours in the best way he/she can yet considering all the different constraints we have. There is not a stereotypical day and even the same person might use the day differently depending on the period, life stage and even day of the week. However, one could assume that most of the people would fall under one of the following six groups of people: 9 to 5 day, workaholic, entrepreneur, unemployed, night job or 2 jobs.

In fact, the way people spend the 24 hours mostly depends on the kind of job they have (or not have) and the number of hours they sleep. Working and sleeping, in fact, generally represent about two thirds of a day if not more. The remaining one third of the day is spent on commuting, eating, preparing and, if any, the spare time is dedicated to hobbies, passions and interests. A clear exception is the day of entrepreneurs – for them, most of the time, there is not a clear-cut difference between the many activities and everything is mixed up.

Did you pay attention to your 24 hours day? Try to plot it on a 24-hour map and see how it looks like. Ask yourself: is this how I want to carry the rest of my life? If not, and you realize you are not giving priority to the big rocks then what can you do to change? Conversely, how do you make sure you keep your current equilibrium?

There is no right or wrong answer to the 24-hours map. But, once you have done the exercise, check whether this is the result you were expecting? If yes, then great keep it up and periodically check how you're doing. Conversely, if the big rocks aren't getting in, what will have to happen so that they do? It might be worth start developing a plan to improve and bring the balance back in your life. As mentioned before, every person has his/her own definition of "live life to the fullest" and his/her own definition of balanced life.

Again, this is about investing the bulk of your time on your biggest rock first! In other words, it is about doing the low priority task faster. My top three tips to save time and help living life to the fullest are listed here below, and in one of the following chapters you will find even 100 tips and tricks that can help you.

Do It Once

"One's objective should be to get it right, get it quick, get it out, and get it over... your problem won't improve with age." – Warren Buffett

Whether related to business or personal life a good decision-making process is instrumental to be more effective in time management. Good *managers* are the ones who can take decisions! Limbo due to the lack of decision making generally means waste of time and resources in general. Good *leaders* are the ones who can make the right decision at the right time and stick to it. In fact, taking a decision is not always enough, if that decision is not right or if it is not taken at the right time and especially if the decision keeps changing. Obviously smart people can change mind but change generally comes with a new set of data or information, variation in landscape/dynamic or because of any other kind of alteration in other related matters. Same is valid for one of the most time-consuming tasks – e-mails – go through them only once: act, archive, delete… but do it only once. Hence, rule #1 is about taking the right decisions at the right time and stick to them (unless something is changing/new info are available).

Right Thing at Right Time

"I try to do the right thing at the right time. They may just be little things, but usually they make the difference between winning and losing." – Kareem Abdul-Jabbar

We tend to execute things as they come (First In First Out) or in function of priority/urgency matrix. Instead, I believe that certain tasks need to be accomplished during specific timeframes which depend on the specific personality and situation. For example, it might take ages to someone writing a report after lunch if this is the busiest time of the day for meetings/requests – on the other hand that person could write it quickly early in the morning when no one is in the office. Or it might not be productive to seek for an approval by a person early in the morning when that person is not in the proper mindset at that time.

Our day could be divided into six parts: morning commute, early hours in the office (no one there!), "official" working hours, evening commute, family time, night work. Our task consists into understanding which kind of work we should do when in order to maximize productivity for each specific and different task Hence, rule #2, find your perfect task/timeframe match.

Be Disciplined

"Self-respect is the fruit of discipline; the sense of dignity grows with the ability to say no to oneself." – Abraham Joshua Heschel

If you don't discipline yourself then others will discipline you. There is always something to do, and there is always someone asking you to do more… which is great. However, set your goal – define what you want to achieve during the day (and in your life!) and put clear start/stop in your agenda for each part of the day so to get the opportunity to achieve your goal. Make it loud and clear and stand for it. Learn how to say "NO". Obviously there will be exceptional days and you need to be flexible but those should be the exception and not the rule. Finally, rule #3, stand for your time.

VINCENZO CARRARA

CHAPTER II

The NEAT Day

"Doing something that is productive is a great way to alleviate emotional stress. Get your mind doing something that is productive." – Ziggy Marley

VINCENZO CARRARA

The NEAT Day

Many of us have a "routine day" and this is often organized around the working hours and the many meetings we have to attend. We try to force fit the rest of our life around and sometimes in between the working hours. Some do it successfully and are satisfied with it, but many others keep struggling for the best balance. Reality is that we should not think about working day and then organize accordingly – we should think about the NEAT day! NEAT is an acronym which stands for: Nourish, Evaluate, Accomplish and Think. Those are the four things we should do every single day in our life.

In this chapter we will explain the meaning of the four blocks and how to possibly organize the day around them.

Nourish

This is maybe the most important block of the day and if you need to select one block as a priority then I would focus on this one. Nourish means providing the right conditions for growth. This is not limited to the physical growth but also to the psychological and any other kind of growth you might think of. Obviously, you need rest and food for your body, but you might need rest and "food" also for your soul, heart and mind. There are moments in the day clearly allocated to feeding the body - though for some people those are not always a priority and sometimes we skip them or don't dedicate quality time to them. However, not everyone clearly defines moments in the day to nurture soul, heart and mind. We don't live to work but work to live, hence remember to holistically nourish yourself every single day. Try to block your agenda to dedicate quality time to nourish your mind, heart and soul too.

Evaluate

The human being is a social animal and as such he keeps exchanging ideas and confronts others. This is the way we evolve and get better. Without exchange and external evaluation there is limited progression. For this reason, it is important to have "evaluation" moments during the day – moments during which we exchange ideas with others and seek their thoughts. We need to keep evaluating what we are doing and whether we are going in the right direction or not. You can call those moments "meetings" but they do not need to be official – you just need to exchange ideas and thoughts with other people to evaluate your thinking. Remember that the best conclusions come from the confrontation between a thesis and its anti-thesis (Hengel – thesis antithesis synthesis). Hence don't be scared by confrontation and evaluation as it generally leads people to better result personally and professionally.

Accomplish

At the end of the day, it is rewarding to think about what we have accomplished hence about what else we can aim at. In order to reach that rewarding moment, however, we need first to accomplish something. The best way to achieve a goal is via planning for it and this is the famous or infamous "to do list". Whether you have a written official list of whether you keep it in your mind, it does not matter. The important is to have clarity about what you want and can achieve during the day and it is even more important to allocate quality time to accomplish that goal. If you don't know what you want to achieve or don't have quality time allocated then, at the end of the day, you will be wondering why you are not moving forward. Hence plan, accomplish and keep moving.

Think

It seems obvious, but it is not actually. During the day we pass from one activity to another and very seldom dedicate quality time to proper thinking. It seems we are concerned about getting bored and we keep trying to fill the "empty spaces" with more or less useful things. Think about your "spare" time and the many things you do in order not to think: listen to music or podcast, reading, talking… those are all great things (by the way part of "nourish") but sometimes it is good to just stop and think.

Clear your mind and dedicate quality time to the things that concern you the most, the problems you want to solve or the things you have achieved, the many more things you still want to do... get out of the "train of life" and get a different perspective.

Those are the four blocks that make a NEAT day. Think thoroughly through and organize each and every single day with those in mind. As mentioned, the "nourish" block might be the one to start from – easy to plan for the body-nourishing moments but make sure to allocate time also to your soul, heart and mind. Then try to have both "accomplish" and "evaluate" moments during the working hours. Finally, if there is time left add "think" moments and if there is no more time then re-evaluate the other three to make time to think! As said, all the four blocks need to be present each single day. You decide how much to dedicate to one vs the others and how to create space but have them all!

CHAPTER III

100 Time Management

Tips and Techniques

"Time management is an oxymoron. Time is beyond our control, and the clock keeps ticking regardless of how we lead our lives. Priority management is the answer to maximizing the time we have." - John C. Maxwell

VINCENZO CARRARA

100 Time Management
Tips and Techniques

Take the time to read this chapter as it might save you lots of time! It might look like a long list of tips and techniques but if you go through it, you will realize how dramatically you can improve your time management skills. It is a bit like learning how to drive a car – at the beginning you have lots of thing to read, study and remember, but then everything will come to you naturally and you'll be able to go anywhere you want. You just need to practice!

In order to simplify the reading, I have divided the 100 time-management tips and techniques into twelve sections: analyze, to-do-list, prioritize, plan, organize, block time, say "NO", downtime, meetings, e-mails social media & similar, tools & systems and others. Every section is independent so that you can decide whether reading only what you believe is most appropriate for you or you can read them all.

ANALYZE

We tend to jump directly into improving planning and defining improvement areas. However, before doing that, we should try to understand what works and what does not work for us. Analysis is actually the base for defining an improvement plan hence worth investing some of your time on it.

1. Take time and plot out what you do every day. Be honest and include everything, even the multiple coffee breaks! It might be painful, but it is instrumental to make more intelligent decisions about how to improve the way you use your time.
2. Every day might be different hence carry a notebook and record all your activities for a week at least.
3. Cut big jobs into small chunks and try to cluster similar activities in blocks (e.g. coffee break, weekly meeting, report writing, lunch, sales pitch…).
4. Make an overall day average about the way you spend your day and underline what drains your time (and/or what drains your energy)
5. Repeat the same exercise for the weekends. Ultimately you might want to make sure you are using the entire week in the best possible way. In fact, depending on your ultimate goal whether about optimizing work-life balance, dedicating more time to family or achieving another specific goal, it might then be necessary to analyze also the weekends.

TO DO LIST

This is most likely the most common tip to help better manage your time. It is kind of obvious – they say, "you get what you measure" and this is valid also for time management. If you don't write down what you want to achieve then you will not achieve it.

6. Make a to-do list electronic or on paper! I prefer on paper as it seems people better assimilate and memorize if it is done in the old good way. Jot down the most important and/or urgent items first and work down from there.
7. Some people like using an organizer. The organizer helps being on top of everything whether, to-do lists, projects, and other miscellaneous items.
8. Create the list before the day unfolds. Do it in the morning or even better, the night before you go to bed.
9. Use down time (e.g. switching-on the PC or waiting for meetings to begin) to update the to-do list or start drafting the new one.
10. While drafting the list, if a task takes less than five minutes, do it right away. You don't want a "shopping list" of hundreds of items that require five mins to be completed. Conversely, put it on the list.
11. Make a time-based to-do list – in other words, include a rough estimate of how much time you'll spend on each item on the list. A simple to-do list is helpful but adding a time dimension can dramatically improve your time effectiveness

as it can help you better prioritizing and also understanding how much you can achieve in a day.

12. Set goals for both the short term and long term as to what you want to accomplish. It might even make more sense for you to have two lists: day specific to-do-list and medium/long term to-do-list.
13. Carry your to-do list with you always and try to keep an eye at it instead of forgetting it in the drawer.
14. Don't think of the totality of your to-do list but take one step at time otherwise you might think you'll never make it... and you'll never make it. Instead tackle one single task at time.
15. For the "big" (high priority and/or urgent) items in the list you might want to schedule reminders or block time in your calendar either in the PC or mobile phone i.e. leverage technology.
16. At the end of the day, review what you've done and make a new list for the next day.

PRIORITIZE

While building the famous (or infamous) to-do-list it is instrumental to associate also priorities. One needs to make sure to accomplish certain task first before moving into others. Conversely, we risk acting first on the task that we like the most which might not necessarily be the most important or urgent.

17. Priorities will ultimately depend on your goal(s). Once you know exactly what you want to achieve you can define which task are the most urgent and/or important.
18. Be ruthless about setting priorities. Make sure that, what you define as important is really imperative and what you define as urgent really needs to be done fast and cannot be postponed.
19. Learn how to differentiate between the important and the urgent. What's important is not always urgent. What's urgent is not always important.
20. Use an A-B-C rating system to assign priorities so that you can grasp the importance of the task at a glance.
21. There is not "D" priority! Always apply the 80/20 rule (20% of effort leads to 80% or results) and get rid of the tasks that don't bring meaningful results (the famous "D" priority).
22. To-do lists tend to get longer and longer to the point where they're unworkable. Have the discipline to keep working always on the most urgent and/or important tasks first.
23. Once you know exactly the priorities (and related time needs), try to understand what can be accomplished within the day and what needs to be postponed and act on consequences (keep turning down things that don't fit into your priorities!).

PLAN

Don't limit your planning to the to-do-list. Have a medium / long term vision that leads to your ultimate objective and plan for it. The medium / long term plan might have quite an impact on the to-do-list.

24. Get an early start! I believe on the fact that "the early bird catches the worm". Early mornings are quiet, and you can get some quality time to think thoroughly through and to develop a solid and robust plan.

25. No matter when, take at least 30 minutes of every day to review your long-term plan and see whether / how this can impact the famous to-do-list. Some people prefer to do this work at night, some do it during commute and others keep updating a "living" list – I do it early morning!

26. Use a calendar, whether electronic or on paper, to keep your plan on track. Some people love electronic calendars synchronized across multiple devices and others prefer the old agenda/calendar. No matter which one you use the importance is to keep it updated and always with you.

27. If possible, try to group related activities – it is more efficient as it might require less back-and-forth between similar tasks.

28. On the other hand, check whether big tasks can be broken down into smaller activities that may be easier to schedule. Some, for example, might not be that urgent or important.

29. Try adding some buffer in your timeline – in other words, try to target to be early. People tend to under estimate the time needed to accomplish tasks hence always better to plan for a bit more time and target to be early.

30. Leave a buffer-time also between tasks. You want to ensure your productivity level is always at the maximum and you need down-time. While taking a break, go for a short walk or perform some other mind-clearing exercise.
31. Before every call and/or meeting, define what you want to achieve and how. Keep the objective in front of you as this will help you getting to the ultimate result and reduce time wasters. If you did not get the expected result evaluate why and how to improve the next time.
32. Identify and limit anything causing a regular, repeated drain your time or energy. Check whether systems or technology can help or whether you can delegate.

ORGANIZE

One of the key factors to success (which relates also to "time management" success) is "focus". In order to be focused one needs to eliminate all distractions and get as much organized as possible. Think about when you play at TETRIS, if you focus you can then better organize the blocks and manage the game faster.

33. Organize and clear the clutter in your workspace. In this way it will be easier to keep focus and don't waste time looking for things. Most importantly keep it so – it is a matter of habit! Keeping your workspace organized will save time while having to re-organize every other month might actually not save you any time.

34. Eliminate all the non-essentials whether from your desk, desktop or anywhere you are. "Focus" is the name of the game and the less distraction you have the faster you'll be able to accomplish the different tasks.
35. Create the business environment that makes you feel more concentrated and productive. Adjust the lighting, turn off your E-mail pop-ups, increase (or lower) the temperature...
36. Keep a clock always visible in front of you or easily accessible. You might get lost in your activity and not realizing how fast time goes.
37. Set reminders "X" minutes before each activity is supposed to end (or start) – leverage technology for that.
38. Schedule similar tasks together if possible especially if the synergies are obvious. It can really streamline the process.
39. Make sure to have a proper filing system for documents and consistently use it.
40. Unsubscribe from e-mail lists if you don't want to receive their content – they are terrible time wasters.
41. During the buffer time in-between activities take note of what achieved and what other tasks you might need to add on the to-do-list… remember to keep the to-do-list always with you.
42. Some people are multi-tasking, but the bulk of people are not able to effectively work on multiple tasks at the same time. If you are among those last then, focus on just one key task

at once. Shut down everything else, clean your desk and do that one thing before start thinking about the next one.
43. Details are important for certain categories and/or jobs but most of the time you might forget about them (remember the 80:20 rule?). Details tend to be a distraction that makes you waste time and become less productive.

BLOCK TIME

We are talking about how to best manage your time and the best way to do that is via putting clear boundaries between you and the rest of the world.

44. Schedule some uninterrupted time each day when you can concentrate on important tasks – I generally do that early morning when finding quality time is relatively easy.
45. Agenda tends to fill fast whatever amount of time you happen to have, and distractions can come easily. Once you set the time blocks, then be disciplined and use the blocks exclusively for the tasks associated.
46. Trying to do everything everyone asks you to do is a recipe for failure. Don't get into the trap of wanting to make everyone happy – set clear boundaries and clarify what you can do and when.
47. Even if you have an "open door" policy you might need (from time to time) to close the door and avoid drop-in visitors. This will give (hopefully) a clear sign that you need some quality time to do some work.

48. Put up a "do not disturb" sign when you absolutely have to get work done.
49. Put a time limit to each task with a clear block in the agenda and stick to it. Do not drag tasks and if you don't have enough time, evaluate whether cancelling other activities or postponing what you have started (depending of priority of other tasks).
50. Schedule demanding tasks for that part of the day when you're at your peak and block time in advance.
51. Schedule time for interruptions. Those are as much important as the "working" time – the interruptions ensure you keep being productive. A good coffee (or tea or walk…) with colleagues or friends can help you being more productive and faster.
52. Practice not answering the phone just because it's ringing and e-mails just because they show up. Plan appropriate time for emails and returning phone calls.
53. Block out other distractions like Facebook and other forms of social media unless you use these tools to generate business.

SAY "NO"

Learning to say "NO" is one of the most difficult and at the same time the most needed skill a manager needs to learn in order to become successful. We have the tendency to make people happy hence we tend to say "YES" to the many requests.

But time is a limited resource, and a "NO" answer, can ultimately help achieving the final objective.

54. Don't take on more than you can handle. When you build your plan and then the to-do-list try to understand whether you have enough capacity. Conversely, evaluate what you need to strike-through i.e. say "NO" in order to achieve your primary daily goal.
55. Everything can be an opportunity, but successful people understand which ones are the biggest and less resource intensive hence say "NO" to the others. Try to evaluate what you can decline!
56. Say "NO" politely, but firmly… and, if you have the time, explain why "NO".
57. Turn off your cell phone and many beepers/pop-ups that inform you about messages. Leverage voice mail messages and even "out-of-office" notes.
58. Say "NO" to social media time wasters. Replace social media bookmarks with work-related sites.
59. Stick to time and say "NO" when people want to drag conversations.

DOWN TIME

We all need down time. Down time should not be seen as a waste of time, but as a source of new energy, inspiration and ultimately a driver of higher productivity (hence better time management).

60. Take mini breaks when you need them during the day to recharge and refocus. Some people advise a break every 90 minutes of work, but do as you believe is the best for you and your body.
61. Stop working (and thinking about work) during the long breaks like the weekends, in the evening and on holiday. This will ensure you're full of energy and still motivated once back at work.
62. Find quality time for meditation or just for a simple and solitary walk. Your mind needs silence to think thoroughly through but also to get re-energized.
63. On the other hand, you might want to leverage the "waiting time". Whether in waiting rooms, lines at the store, commute, etc. you might want to use that time to get things done. You might update your famous to-do-list or you might listen to podcast or might clean up your inbox...
64. Remember to sleep at least 7-8 hours! Sleep deprivation is a known torture method and you don't want to torture yourself. You need a good sleep amount in order to be productive. Most of the people need 7-8 hour, you might need less or more... just listen to your body.

MEETINGS

Meetings are supposed to help a team accomplishing certain objectives while in many cases they are just a forum for people to show off or just to feel useful. Many companies tackle meetings in different ways depending also on the specific company culture, but most of them follow similar guidelines.

65. Do you really need that meeting? Can it be solved with a phone call? Often, we jump into organizing meetings when a situation can be simply solved in other more effective ways.
66. Set clear meeting expectations (i.e. meeting scope) and share them with the team before the meeting. Don't meet just to talk but clarify what you are trying to achieve and keep it present during the entire meeting … maybe write it on a wall?
67. Provide an agenda and a meeting process/flow (ideally with timing for each block) so that everyone is aware of (time) constraints and what is expected from them.
68. Send pre-work if needed and make sure this is done prior the meeting
69. Stick to the schedule and ask (politely) people to do the same.
70. Remove distractions! If not needed ask people to switch off their mobile phones but especially their PC!!!
71. Some companies have meetings standing up or in uncomfortable positions so that they make sure people go straight to the point instead of "making shows".
72. Park any topic which might arise that will not lead to achieving the meeting objective or that cannot be solved on the spot.

73. Don't attend every single meeting you are invited to. Try to understand whether your presence is really needed and why – otherwise just skip it.
74. Write a meeting summary within 24 hours with clear agreements and especially next steps so that people know what they need to do and keep things moving

E-MAILS, SOCIAL MEDIA & SIMILAR

E-mails and social media are by now instrumental to most kind of businesses. However, if not handled carefully the might become the first reason for failure.

75. Deal with e-mails at set times each day – generally once or twice a day is sufficient.
76. Open e-mails only once and act on them straight away (if possible). People tend to open and close e-mails and then re-read them which is a complete waste of time.
77. Use and ask to use clear subject lines. It must be clear from the subject whether your specific action is required (and whether urgent) or whether it is just for info.
78. Ask not to be in "cc" and get out of long chains of e-mails if not needed – another time waster – be polite but do ask for it!
79. When other things get really urgent and you're tight on time, then ignore email completely. If someone is really desperate to reach you, he/she will then call you!

80. Get into the habit of switching off email whenever you can, even if this is only for 15 minutes or 30 minutes at a time.
81. Leverage out of office note while on vacation to ask people to send e-mails to you only if really needed. You might even try deleting all messaged received while out of the office – if really important they might write back or call you.
82. Be aware of amount of time you spend browsing Twitter, News or other social media sites as this can be one of the biggest drains on productivity. Try monitoring time spent on those and see whether appropriate for your plan/objective.
83. If you're using social media for business, similarly to e-mails, allocate specific time during the day for those tasks. You don't have to be there all the time and you might also leverage some tools/systems.
84. Keep your watch on the desk and keep track of how much time you spend on social media and similar.

TOOLS & SYSTEMS

There is a myriad of tools available in the market – some are for free others require a subscription. Today even more than in the past we have the chance to leverage apps, for example, that can simplify our life and reduce the time we spend on certain tasks.

85. If part of your day involves routine repetitive tasks, keep records of how long they take and then try to understand whether some tools and/or systems might help you automate.

For example, Buffer is a great tool to automate posting on social media.

86. Use the technology to get rid of most of the paper in your life – it is generally faster to retrieve documents in your hard drive rather than in your cabinet (assuming you organize both well). So, when possible try to work with electronic documents.
87. Try some of the many scheduling software that allow you to keep a calendar, "to-do' lists, and phone and address books on your computer. You might even leverage project collaboration tools.
88. Track the time spent with tools like Egg Timer (simple online countdown timer). Great for example to give you a beep once the max time allowed on Social Media has been reached.
89. Some people are great at multi-tasking – if you are among them try using double screens. I generally actively work on one screen and keep the other one on e-mails and other messaging apps. It might be distracting for some, but if done properly, it increases productivity (e.g. proper use of e-mail subjects…).
90. Leverage instant messaging apps – those might be faster than e-mails also because require less formal introductions to topics and requests.
91. Search for solutions to problems outside – there are tons of blogs that can help you finding fast a solution before even

thinking about organizing a meeting. Depending on the specific topics you might refer to different specific/technical sources or to more generic sites as QUORA.

OTHERS

There are a series of other consideration that can help you with time management – some might be more specific to the individual person other might apply to anyone.

92. Remember the triangle with "quality", "cost" and "time" at the three opposite corners? Then if you want to save time try to understand whether you can compromise on the other two elements.
93. It is known that a healthy lifestyle drives higher work productivity. Hence try to get enough sleep, exercise and eat healthy to boost energy levels and drive up productivity.
94. Learn how to delegate, wherever and whenever you can whether internally or externally (i.e. outsource). Sometimes you might even get better quality work!
95. Always keep a notebook or some tool to record your thoughts and ideas. Those generally come in the less expected time especially solutions to problems. If you are able to jot them down, you will not have to think about them again (assuming you can re-think that very same solution).
96. Turn key tasks into habits. The more you do the better you'll become. As for driving a car – at the beginning you have lots

of thing to read, study and remember but then everything will come to you naturally… you just need to practice!

97. Some people prefer continuity and don't really need a long break in between working weeks. Those people might find useful working a couple of hours during the week-end so to ensure that there is no down and up peaks in work.

98. Celebrate accomplishments … especially the big ones. It might seem a small frugal thing, but it does actually help motivating you and keep energy level high.

99. Sometimes, it's okay to procrastinate. It might sound counter-intuitive but i) some problems do actually solve by themselves with time and ii) sometimes it is better not to react on the emotions but calm down first.

100. Remember that it's impossible to get everything done, but if you start from the most important and urgent you will then get closer to your ultimate objective!

Those are my 100 time-management tips and techniques! I hope you find them useful and let me close this chapter with Warren Buffett quote *"No matter how great the talent or efforts, some things just take time. You can't produce a baby in one month by getting nine women pregnant."*

CHAPTER IV

Just Say NO - Save TIME

"Too many of us fail to fulfill our needs because we say no rather than yes, or perhaps later in life, yes when we should say no." - William Glasser

Just Say NO - Save TIME

One of the first words we learn is "NO" – a very powerful word that unfortunately we tend to forget as we grow up. Some people might learn it once again when they become parents as this is one of the first words we say to the kids. In general, however, we use it less and less as we grow up. There seems to be some differences across geographies and cultures, but overall as we grow we become faster in saying "yes" and we tend to reduce the "no" occasions.

"Half of the troubles of this life can be traced to saying yes too quickly and not saying no soon enough" - Josh Billings.

Generalizing, American and Germans tend to be the most frank and direct in showing a disagreement while Asian tend to be most reticent to using the word "no" and Italians tend to be indirect. Lots of generalization but the point is that, over time, we learn to please people and say "yes" instead of "no". What we don't realize is that via saying "yes" to something or someone, at the same time, we say "no" to something else. Conversely via saying "no" we can create new opportunities

"What you don't do determines what you can do" - Tim Ferriss. Saying "yes" might mean spending time on things that are not relevant and meaningful or in other words we might waste time! Hence just saying "no" might actually help us saving time.

"Say no to everything, so you can say yes to the one thing" — Richie Norton. We could change our life and give it more meaning via spending time on things and with people that are more meaningful to us... we just need to say "no" and simplify our life!

"...there are often many things we feel we should do that, in fact, we don't really have to do. Getting to the point where we can tell the difference is a major milestone in the simplification process" — Elaine St. James. The challenge consists into learning how to say "no". The business man Cole Harmonson *says, "It takes effort to say no when our heart and brains and guts and, most important, pride are yearning to say yes. Practice"*. We grow up with the conviction that a "yes" is more polite and helpful than a "no" and changing mindset at a later stage is not that easy. Mahatma Gandhi used to say, *"A 'No' uttered from the deepest conviction is better than a 'Yes' merely uttered to please, or worse, to avoid trouble"*. So how do we change and start saying "no"? I would advise to follow a five steps approach.

The five steps approach to say "no"

1. Till when we don't realize that *"When you say no to the wrong people, it opens up the space for the right people to*

come in." (Joe Calloway) then we will not take any action. Hence the first step consists into acknowledging that a "no" might be more helpful to us than a "yes".

2. Once we accept this, then we can move to the next step: learning how to say "no". As mentioned before, every culture has its own way to manage and accept disagreement and depending on where you are and with whom you interact, you might use a different message in order to get your "no" through without hampering the relationship. If in doubt, try to look at the situation from the other person's cultural perspective and just say "no" with your heart and explain the reason why you are saying so. This is exactly the same way parents do (or should od) with their children. In this way you might find a common ground and create win-win situation for both parties.

3. The third step is about managing the instinctive reaction – we are generally very fast in saying "yes" and sometimes we need to go back and make corrections to address our original decision. The executive Tom Friel *says, "We need to learn the slow 'yes' and the quick 'no'"*. Take your time to answer and think whether that "yes" is worth your commitment and especially your time.

4. Stick to your decision! Not everyone can accept a "no" hence people might try to convince you otherwise after your first reaction. If you do really believe on your "no" than hold onto that and don't change your mind just because the other

party insists. *"Once you have made up your mind, stick to it; there is no longer any 'if' or 'but'"* - Napoleon Bonaparte. They might convince you that saying "yes" is not really a big burden for you but this is not true. The "yes" accumulates very easily and before you realize your day will be full of many little things that don't make you happy.

5. There is also a fifth step which could, instead, be the first one. This is about understanding what your priorities are hence be prepared to answer with an appropriate "yes" or "no". Instead having to reflect and improvise on the spot (which might always happen) it is better to have a crystal-clear idea of what matters the most in your life. *"You have to decide what your highest priorities are and have the courage pleasantly, smilingly, and non-apologetically – to say "no" to other things. And the way to do that is by having a bigger yes burning inside."* – Stephen Covey. Make a list of what are the most important things and people in your life but also start building an "ignore list". The "ignore list" should be your starting point as it will make it easier to say "no" to certain things. *"Information overload (on all levels) is exactly WHY you need an "ignore list". It has never been more important to be able to say "No"* — Mani S. Sivasubramanian

If you start following the above process, you'll realize that you can actually have more time to dedicate to what matters the most to you. It is about being selective, a bit selfish and filling the life jar with the biggest stones first.

"When you say YES to others, make sure you are not saying NO to yourself" – Paulo Coelho.

The day is still made of 24 hours and about one third is (or should be) spent sleeping which means only 16 hours are left for you to accomplish what you want. Start from defining the first "no" you will say today and use the spare time to celebrate this achievement – this will trigger some motivation and help you doing more frequently. Watch-out though at not becoming the "no" man/woman but rather focus the "no" on the non-meaningful and relevant matters.

Remarkably this is valid also in business – the same challenges and the same process can be followed in the business environment. *"The art of leadership is saying no, not saying yes. It is very easy to say yes"* - Tony Blair. Sometimes a "yes" instead of a "no" could hinder the magnitude of success no matter how we define it. *"The difference between successful people and really successful people is that really successful people say no to almost everything"* - Warren Buffet. In fact, success is about focus and saying no is at the forefront of it. *"Focusing is about saying no"* - Steve Jobs.

CHAPTER V

Delegate Meaning and Techniques

"Surround yourself with the best people you can find, delegate authority, and don't interfere as long as the policy you've decided upon is being carried out." - Ronald Reagan

VINCENZO CARRARA

Delegate Meaning and Techniques

The word "delegate" comes from Latin de-legare which literally means "send with a task". Nowadays more commonly defined as the act of entrusting a task to another person (generally a more junior person). As such, the delegation act implies a trust relationship between two people in which one person gives a task to the other one. Hence, only when a trust relationship is established between the two parties then an act of delegation might happen. It is very important to underline the trust factor as this is the main difference between the act of delegation and the act of assigning a work/task. Delegation means sharing authority, responsibility and accountability.

Then why do we need to delegate? And when and what do we need to delegate? There are essentially two reasons why people should delegate: either because lack of time or because other people might do the work better (or faster or cheaper). This is valid for both personal life and in business. Mastering the different delegation techniques can even be instrumental for the success of a person no matter of how he/she defines it.

What would happen if, instead, people would not delegate? Consequences are quite straightforward. The number of hours in a day is still twenty-four hence without delegating there are only a certain number of things one person can do. This means that if a person does not delegate, then either the work does not get done (or other task are de-prioritized), gets done in a sub-optimal way or the person who's not delegating might reaches a "burnout".

No matter how efficient and masterful people are at their job, there are only so many tasks they can accomplish within a day. This means that, at a certain point, delegation becomes paramount in order to achieve more in a day. Understanding what to delegate, when and to whom, is then what will drive success vs failure. As such, delegation is a critical skill for everyone but especially for entrepreneurs and leaders in charge of big or complex structures / businesses. Remarkably when properly done, delegation is also a very powerful motivational tool for the team. As previously mentioned, the act of delegating implies a trust relationship hence when people get a delegation, then they will understand that they are trusted thus valued.

"Get the right people on the bus, the wrong people off the bus, and the right people in the right seats." - Jim Collins - Good to Great.

As Jim Collins mentioned, it is not just a matter of hiring good people but also about having them doing the "right" things. This is valid for the team but even more for self. Sometimes we are our worst enemy – many of us believe that we can do faster and/or better than anyone else, but unfortunately, this is not always the case. We should make sure that the work gets allocated to the most skilled people for that specific task. In this way we could not only increase the amount of achievements but also improve the overall results we can obtain in a determined period of time.

In a nutshell, delegation might not only save time, but it could also drive better results for self and/or the team. While it is not always evident or easy, delegation needs to be carefully planned. Hence how do people delegate? The secret lays in finding the perfect combination between tasks to delegate, right people to delegate to and style of delegation. At the beginning this might be a quite cumbersome process and accomplishing tasks might take longer. However, over time the more one practices the easier and faster it will become.

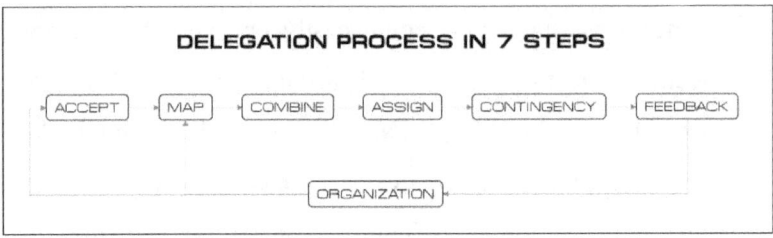

1. **Accept**. The first and most obvious step is the "acceptance" – acceptance that an act of delegation is inevitable at a certain point. No matter whether we are unemployed, entrepreneurs or employees – there is always a point at which we will need friend, family or a team to achieve more or better results. If one has never delegated in the past, the first time it might be difficult hence it could be worth starting with a single, low priority task. Once the very first task is accomplished then it might start being easier to delegate more and bigger tasks. This might help accepting the delegation act as a method needed to increase the productivity and then he/she can move to the other steps of this process.

2. **Map**. After having accepted the fact that delegation might become a must, then we can start identifying the tasks that need to be delegated. This is about mapping all the tasks we generally accomplish and the ones we are not yet capable of doing because either lack of time or competences. First identify the ones that are repetitive or relatively easily accomplished – like the ones that could be done by a (virtual) assistant. One could easily delegate, for example, agenda, meeting and travel arrangements. Then, move toward the highly complex and specialized like legal work or accounting tasks. Finally evaluate the ones in between which generally are more difficult to hand-off. Remember that delegation might work in any direction – one might delegate

to peers, managers and direct reports within an organization but even outside the own company. Don't be concerned about delegating up or sideways – just find the best way to do it effectively. While building the "to delegate" list think also about what you do not want and should not delegate. For example, tasks of a highly sensitive nature which, depending on the size of the company, might relate to salary reviews or customer relationship for example.

3. **Combine**. The most sensitive part of the delegation process is about finding the perfect combination between task and the most appropriate person to accomplish it. As we mentioned at the beginning, delegating is about asking someone we trust to do something for us – this means that the first thing to look at is "trust". However, this does not mean that we need to find people who we generically "trust", but rather people who we can trust to accomplish the specific task. For example, we might generically trust our partner but I'm not sure we would trust him/her for doing a surgical operation on us (unless he/she a surgeon). In other words, once you have listed all the tasks to delegate try to understand who in your team (or even outside your team) you would trust to accomplish that specific activity independently from his or her role/level in the organization. This implies that you know your team and their strengths and opportunity areas. Conversely, if you are not sure, involve the team and ask them who feels confident and

motivated to accomplish the specific task. Never forget, though, capacity of other team members – make sure not to overload any of them.

4. **Assign**. The way the act of delegation is executed is also fundamental to the achievement of the desired result. You don't want them to just execute your "recipe" because they will never achieve the result you expect. You want your people to achieve the ultimate end-result; you want their complete commitment, motivation and engagement. The only way to achieve that is via finding a win-win solution. You want to delegate a task and your people want to be valued, develop and grow. This is a very sensitive step hence few considerations in this context:

   a. *Delegate vs Assign*. Have a proper briefing session and start from the big picture to then go into the details of how their task fits in it. Explain why the task needs to be accomplished within the specific timeframe. In order to further motivate explain also why you have specifically chosen that person to accomplish the task (emphasize his/her skills). Finally, before moving forward ensure that they have positive feeling about the task and if not try to understand and address any concern.

   b. *Set clear expectations*. Set very clear expectations both in terms of results expected and in term of time for the delivery and underline any flexibility in either of them.

Don't get into the temptation of describing in a detailed way how to achieve the ultimate end-result – no one want to be just an executer – focus on the final result expected and help them only if they seek for more details. Be clear on the measures you will look at in order to understand whether the task has been accomplished successfully.

c. *Enable*. Before letting the person work on the task make sure he/she has everything needed to accomplish it successfully. If this is not the case, then evaluate what's needed hence how to enable him/her. Flag the fact that your door is always open in case new roadblocks should arise – this might be especially valid if you are delegating first time or to junior people. Finally, don't forget that you are delegating not just a task but also authority – your people need to feel 100% empowered if you want to achieve the best results.

d. *Get out of the way*. Once you have done the above then your own task is about disappearing! Don't micro-manage, don't check continuously developments, don't wander around … all those actions will ultimately de-motivate your people. Remember you are delegating to a person you trust hence there is no need to be around and if you feel the need then this means you don't trust that person … hence delegate to someone else! This does not mean that you should never ever check – especially if you are delegating a long-term project, you might have some check points along the way. The important is to make these checkpoints clear when you set expectations so that the person does not take it as micro-managing but as a way to share ideas and check whether there is need for help.

5. **Contingency Plan**. Things might always turn bad and having a contingency plan is not a bad idea especially when delegating critical task for the first time or to people with limited expertise (which should not happen). However, before taking control back try to understand whether the person you delegated to can still fix the situation. This could be an amazing learning opportunity for him/her but also for you. Only if she/he cannot fix it, then it will be your turn to jump in and solve the situation.

6. **Feedback**. Upon completion of the task it is always a good habit to review the entire process together. There are lots of learning that could be gathered and be beneficial to anyone in the company or organization in general. If the task has been accomplished successfully don't be shy with praise and compliments because those are great motivators. Conversely if there have been some hiccups then be direct (with tact) and flag improvement areas – you want to make sure that the next time this task will be accomplished successfully.

7. **Organization**. This is the moment to (re)assess the organization. After having delegated some tasks you might

be in a better position to evaluate your people and see who you can trust for specific task (or not). This actually starts at the hiring moment – when interviewing candidates always wonder whether you would delegate specific tasks or even functions to the person. In case of doubt don't hire as it would be totally useless to have a person in the team who you don't trust hence to whom you would not delegate work.

Remember, delegation is crucial no matter whether you are an employee, business owner or even a mother/father. There is nothing wrong in leveraging the experience and expertise of others to get better results and more time for self. The sooner you learn how to delegate the faster you will get more time for yourself. Finally, learn to ask! Some of us tend to do everything by themselves because don't dare to ask or don't want to bother others. I'm guilty on this, but we can learn to ask… because if you don't ask you don't get!

VINCENZO CARRARA

CHAPTER VI

Panic and Procrastination

"Imagination only comes when you privilege the subconscious, when you make delay and procrastination work for you." - Hilary Mantel

VINCENZO CARRARA

Panic and Procrastination

The American business magnate Warren Buffett says: *"One's objective should be to get it right, get it quick, get it out, and get it over... your problem won't improve with age."* This statement makes sense most of the time and, as such, people wisely advise not to procrastinate. However, in certain situations, procrastination can actually help solving problems or avoid creating new ones.

Everyone knows that procrastination does not help people or companies moving forward. In fact, by definition, procrastination is the act of delaying or postponing something. Hence how could this possibly help? Most of the time, in fact, it does not help. In few cases, conversely, procrastination might help moving forward and in rare cases it can lead to an even faster or cheaper solution. Difficult to believe! You have been "fighting" procrastination since you discovered its meaning and the related impact on the developments and now you might discover that you can leverage procrastination? Yes, you can!

"It is early morning in NYC and James is working hard on a new development. Suddenly an unexpected phone call. The plant manager informs James that the production line in China has a problem and the product will be delivered late. Panic. A rush of adrenaline. The first thought of James goes to the reaction of his manager and especially the one of the CEO of the company. His career is over! James needs to act and he needs to do it fast – there is no time for procrastination!

Shortly after the call, James organizes a crisis meeting and invites the multifunctional team to discuss possible solutions. A team of fifteen people rushes in every direction, they meet and call internal and external stakeholders. Several meetings take place during the day and James desperation increases from one unsuccessful meeting to another.

It is late evening and James has not been able to find a solution yet. He decides it is time to inform his manager and the company CEO. This is James worst professional day and he believes his last day in the company. He is a good steward though hence he prepares all the needed documentation and call the meeting with his manager and company CEO. The issue is revealed and the reaction of top management is even worse than expected. James is out!

It is 8pm and in the office there are only few people still working, including top management. James telephone rings again but this time he is not there to answer. The telephone keeps ringing and finally someone decides to take that call. It is the plant manager calling from China. He and his team have been working all night on the production line. They have fixed the problem and the product will be delivered on time!

Unfortunately, James is not there to hear the great news and an entire multi-functional team has wasted a full day working with internal and external stakeholders to find a solution to a not existing problem."

Brief story to say that sometimes problems solve by themselves and procrastinating a bit might be more fruitful than taking immediate action. The above seems to be an extreme and unique case but if you pay attention to your business and personal life you'll notice lots of conceptually similar cases. We need to keep moving and we need to take decisions, but, when facing a problem, we need first to make sure it is a real problem. Procrastinating on a problem to evaluate it before acting might hence be a good thing.

The important watch-out for people who tend to procrastinate is not to use it as an excuse for not taking decisions. The procrastinators tend not to act or make decisions on things they don't like, don't know, they fear or when they do not want to be controversial. In those cases, leveraging "panic" might help moving forward and overcome procrastination. Panic, in fact, is the one feeling that can help procrastinators making decisions and move forward.

This is to say that panic might help the "naturally born" procrastinators but it might be detrimental to the other people. Hence, if you are a procrastinator, try to leverage panic to move forward – conversely, never give up to panic and rush decisions when encountering problems because panic might mislead you and it could lead you taking actions that are actually counterproductive. Take your time!

"There's nothing wrong with procrastination. Or is there? I'll leave it to you to decide, but only if you have the time." - Craig Brown

CHAPTER VII

10 Activities for Commute Time

"Time goes on. So whatever you're going to do, do it. Do it now. Don't wait." - Robert De Niro

VINCENZO CARRARA

10 Activities for Commute Time

Lots of people commute every day from home to the office and sometimes for long hours. The commute is seen by many as a waste of time and often as a needed compromise to get a good job and a valuable place of living. Commute hours and days accumulate over time and they might become a relevant part of an entire lifetime. Hence the question – how can we get the most out of the daily commute?

There are lots of things that can be done during the commute time. It all depends on the way people commute though. Some people might drive hence need hands-free activities while others use public transportation and might not have access to telephone line and/or internet. No matter how people commute there is always something that can be done to make it more productive and worthwhile. The next section underlines our top ten activities to do while commuting.

Podcast

This is the most evident activity that could help improving the day. Most podcasts are either educational or entertaining. No matter which one people choose, the important is to plan for it and make sure that the podcast is entirely downloaded so that there is no need for connection... and don't forget to charge the battery! I personally love the TED Talks podcasts but this is a personal choice.

Clean-up

It is never a good time for cleaning up. People have always higher priority things to do hence why not taking advantage of the commute? This might relate to cleaning up your bag, your old-style agenda, and your photos on the mobile phone or even the hundreds of e-mails that are waiting for you in the inbox.

Drafts

For the people who leverage the "comfortable" public transportation, the commute could be a good time to make drafts. It is, actually, the perfect time to draft that e-mail or note that requires some attention and that needs "sleeping over" so not to create disasters. Some might want to use this time to draft blog posts, articles and even books – I did write this book entirely during my commute time in the New York subway!

Think

During commute time people are free from any office or home constraint. Their mind is free to wander around and they can think thoroughly through. This is the time to ideate and innovate. Ideas, however, disappear fast hence make sure to have a piece of paper or a mobile phone to take note before it is too late.

Read & Listen

The commute is the "decompressing chamber" between office and home (or vice versa). Every person has his/her own way to transition from office to home. Some like to listen to music others might read a book or play cross words and Sudoku. The important is to find the activity that helps you the most in transitioning and start fresh the new chapter in the daily routine.

To Do List

The famous (or infamous) "to do list" is also part of my top ten. I do believe on the "to do list" – not necessarily on a very detailed and complicated one but at least on a quick and rough collection of priorities. This can be easily done on a commute and can dramatically help achieving what people are aiming at. In this context see also our other chapter "100 time-management tips and techniques" if not already done.

Dream & Plan

Routine is an ugly beast. It takes our time and minds and we often forget to dream and dream big. While commuting there is nothing wrong on dreaming. This is the time to unleash your creative mind and think about the infinite possibilities. But a dream is just a dream unless you start drafting a plan to materialize it so leverage the commute to dream and plan for it.

Talk

Talk to a stranger. During commute (if on public transportation) you have the opportunity to meet people with very different background and perspectives. Those are the most enriching encounters both from a personal as well as business perspective. One never knows who he/she might be talking to and the incredible amount of insight and joy he/she might get from that unexpected conversation. Dare to talk!

Observe

Close your eyes and think about what you listen and smell during your commute – open your eyes and observe. Most people remember only few things. People are generally so immersed in their thoughts or other activities that forget to pay attention to the world around them. There are tons of things happening and we can learn from the world around us via just observing with attention. Both people, events, nature, sounds and even objects can be a source of inspiration and learning. Do look carefully.

Meditate!

Life is like a train, we jump in and we keep going often without wondering where we are going. Where are you going? Is this the life you want to live? Leverage the commute time to think and (re)evaluate what you are doing. Life is too short to realize only at the end that we are heading in the wrong direction.

By the way, those top ten things are valid not just for commute time but also for any occasion during which we need to wait. Think about the waiting room at the doctor or public office or even while queuing at the supermarket. Don't waste your time!

CHAPTER VIII

10 Reasons to Wear a Wristwatch

"When a guy takes off his coat, he's not going to fight. When a guy takes off his wristwatch, watch out!" - Al McGuire

10 Reasons to Wear a Wristwatch

You don't actually need a wristwatch! People have been living for generations without wrist watches. People have been obsessed by the measure of the passage of time since ever, but the wrist watch has been introduced only in the last 200 years. Nowadays there is even less of a reason to use a wrist watch considering that time can be measured by the widespread use of mobile phones. Hence why people still use a wrist watch? And why you do need one in case you don't have it yet!

There are essentially ten reasons why you need a wrist watch. In certain cases, you even don't really have a choice, in others you might still decide not to use a wrist watch but you might need to make some compromises. The following sections underline those ten reasons.

Style or Status Statement

The wrist watch is, definitely, a key fashion accessory. It completes the look of a person and helps defining the personality in a more compelling way. The watch becomes a part of the person identity at such extent that some people feel "naked" if not wearing a wrist watch. For certain people or occasions the watch is used as a mere complement to the overall look – in other situations the wrist watch can be the "main piece" and be used as a statement: a style statement or even a status symbol.

Diving

There are no mobile phones (yet) enough resistant to water pressure to be used for diving. For this reason, divers are still limited to the use of wrist watches to measure the passage of time. This is not a choice but a must as they have to know how long their immersion is lasting.

Convenience

The key reason for the invention of the wrist watch was its convenience. The possibility to check the time hands free with just a flip of the wrist was, in fact, the key driver for this development. This is very handy in a series of occasions like when driving a motorbike or car and it can even be a must in other situations like when doing certain type of sport activities (can you imagine a referee having to check his mobile phone during a match?). The only watch-out is not to check the time while having a filled glass in the same hand!

Less distracting than phones

Sometimes you just need to know the time. For those occasions a wrist watch is the best companion – it gives you the time and no excuse for further distractions. On the other hand, as soon as people check their mobile phone for reading the time, they will also discover that there are X email messages unanswered or Y updates to do or Z notifications on whatever social media app present on the mobile phone. This will ultimately lead to a waste of time.

Autonomy

Wrist watches do not need to be charged every day - with the exception of the few that use a manual winding movement. Their incredible autonomy can be very useful in certain context (e.g. military in the field) or for certain professions (e.g. explorers).

Allowed everywhere

Wrist watches are still allowed anywhere and in certain situations they are the only tool that can be used to measure the passage of time. For example, many schools are now forbidding the use of mobile phones and most prohibit their use in the final exams halls. Similarly, many hospitals forbid the use of mobile phones in many areas and doctors can only rely on wall/wrist-watches.

Direction

There is no need for special app or for a compass to understand the direction. A normal watch and even better a 24-hour watch can easily indicate the direction.

On the 24-hour watches, for example, once the wearer orientates the watch in a way to align the hour hand with the sun, the north direction is toward the bottom of the watch dial (see image). This is obviously not a necessity for everyone, yet it can be handy for certain people.

Heirloom

Heirloom might be a big word for most of the wrist watches currently in the market, yet it might apply to the high-end ones. For all others, even if the watch might not be passed from one generation to the other we would expect it to last many years. The same cannot be said for the mobile phones that become obsolete in a couple of years (or faster). In other words, the wrist watches tend to have a longer lasting intrinsic value.

Relationship with time

Watches are meant to measure time and, as such, they establish a close relationship between the wearer and the time dimension. They give a perception of time at a glance and they might impact the way people approach life. For example, the single handed 24-hour watches will give a total different perception of time vs a more traditional three hands 12-hour watch.

Just because we love them!

Some people fall in love with watches in the same way others fall in love with cars or other accessories or pieces of technology. Watches are time machines and they are the ultimate result of thousands of years of research and innovation. They are a piece of history on a wrist.

In conclusions, love them or hate them, wrist watches are here to stay. They might keep evolving over time, but they will remain a loyal companion to many of us nostalgic or not. Now you only need to choose which one to get next.

CHAPTER IX

CLUB 24 - 24 hour watch enthusiasts

"Everybody has 24 hours and the question is, what do you do with your 24 hours? That's what makes everybody equal." - Stedman Graham

VINCENZO CARRARA

CLUB 24 - 24 hour watch enthusiasts

A wristwatch is not for everybody. According to two separate consumer studies, only about the 79 percent and 86 percent of the population respectively in U.S. and U.K. own wristwatches. As per the U.S. study, 76 percent of wristwatch owners claim to have an analog watch and most of the time it is based on the 12-hour system; hours are indicated by a rotating hand from one to twelve twice-a-day.

We grow up with the 12-hour system and get used to it over time. We are so used to it that we can even read a watch without any numbers or markings on it. However, the 12-hour system is neither the most intuitive nor the first system that has been introduced to measure the passage of time. In fact, other systems exist and one of the most common is based on a 24-hour cycle. In those watches the hand which indicates the hours makes a complete rotation in 24 hours — yes, only one rotation per day.

Those watches are used by few people, but the trend is growing, and more companies are developing 24-hour watches. The question is: who is part of the "Club 24"? the club of the lovers of 24-hour watches.

Can anyone benefit from these watches and join Club 24? I believe that a 24-hour watch is a much more intuitive way to measure the passage of time and that a 24-hour wristwatch can brings a lot of benefits once people get used to the new system.

In the following sections, I did cluster the people that would specifically benefit from a 24-hour watch. Though I also believe that the adoption of a 24-hour watch could be beneficial to a much broader audience.

Club 24 is essentially made of seven groups of people: pilots and astronauts, explorers, submariner personnel and people with similar work shifts, planners and entrepreneurs, "alternative" people, soldiers, and people who do "precision" work and radio operators or UTC users in general.

Pilots / Astronauts

Long distance airplane pilots and astronauts travel across multiple time zones; thus a 12-hour watch might bring some confusion on whether the time refers to day or night hours.

Similarly, people who don't have access to natural light like miners and underground workers or people that are located in the

Polar regions might have the same challenge. In those situations, a 24-hour watch can prevent time confusion.

Some of the 24-hour wristwatches have a crystal-clear and visual separation between day and night. For example, the Botta Design Uno 24 as well the Airnautic by Ocean 7 both have a clear color separation between day and night with the top part of the dial in a clear color (6:00 to 18:00) to represent the day and the bottom part of the dial in a darker color (18:00 to 6:00) to represent night.

The Frederique Constant Manufacture Tourbillon is not a 24-hour watch, but it still helps with avoiding the above confusion. This watch is a bit anomalous as it showcases a normal 12-hour cycle, but it has also a sub-dial with a double-ended hand — sun and moon icons at the two ends — which clearly indicates whether the time refers to the 12-day hours or the 12-night hours.

Explorers

An explorer is a person who investigates unknown regions, traveling through an unfamiliar country or area in order to learn about it. Often, explorers get in places where it is not easy to find orientation (e.g. deserts) and/or distinguish the difference between day and night (e.g. speleologists).

For those people a 24-hour watch might help not just because the distinction between day and night hours, but also because those watches are immediate compass. In fact, via pointing the hour hand toward the sun one can find the North position where the 24-hours mark is. This is valid for any 24-hour watch and there is no easier way to combine a compass with a watch.

Submariner Personnel

For years, sailors serving aboard submarines followed a different day, in terms of number of daily hours, in comparison to the rest of the world. Aboard United States submarines personnel used to have 18-hour work cycles: six hours work, six hours maintenance and entertainment and six hours sleeping. In other words, their day was made of 18 hours and the logic was that it was easier for sailors to give their undivided attention to the electronic equipment if the work shift was only six hours.

Luckily, since December 2014 the Navy started the transition to a 24-hour day in three shifts of eight hours each. Not everyone on board, however, has the same 24-hour shift, so a careful schedule planning is needed, and a 24-hour watch is almost instrumental for a correct implementation of the new schedule. In fact, the ideal watch for the personnel would be a 24-hour watch in which it is possible to divide the dial into three parts of eight hours and those parts can move depending on the schedule.

Planners / Logistic professional / Entrepreneurs

Planners and entrepreneurs are masters in time management. In fact, time is one of the most important and limited resource to look after. Seeing the entire day at a glance in a wristwatch is paramount for perfectly managing the daily schedule! The 24-hour watch gives a totally new perspective and helps understand how time is used compared to how it should actually be used. Interestingly to note, the 24-hour system is the one that has been used to standardize and harmonize time planning across different geographies driven by the expansion of the railroad — this is because this system was valued as the best for planning purpose.

"Alternative" people

There are two groups of people that we would define "alternative": people who want to have a different, no rush lifestyle and people who just want to be different. Both groups believe that a 24-hour watch can help them. There are companies that claim that a 24-hour watch can change the way people live and they target the first group of people.

A U.S. study revealed that 30% of the population sees the watch as a fashion accessory or piece of jewelry. As such the wrist watch is another element of differentiation for the people that want to stand out from the crowd. There are myriads of different kinds of unusual and unique watches that could address this objective and the 24-hour watches are among the most unique. In fact, only few people are willing to change from a 12-

hour system to a 24-hour system which keeps these watches exclusive.

Army / Health Professionals / "Precision" jobs

Some professions require an unmistakable time precision. This is the case for army personnel, police officers, doctors and more. None of these people can make mistakes in the definition of time because the consequences might be dramatic.

Confusing 11 a.m. for 11 p.m. in a police case, in a military attack or operation is a very serious thing. Hence these professionals should use 24-hour watches in order to prevent such possible mistakes. Considering the peculiarity of their job, the structure of the 24-hour watch will also most likely need to be super solid and robust (consider the army) and water resistant (think about what can happen to a doctor or surgeon).

Radio Operators / UTC users in general

UTC stands for Coordinated Universal Time and is the primary time standard by which the world regulates clocks and time. In general UTC is the time standard used in aviation (e.g. for flight plans and air traffic control clearances), weather forecasts and maps to avoid confusion about time zones and daylight-saving time.

The International Space Station also uses UTC as a time standard. Another group of people that uses this standard is the amateur radio operators who often schedule their radio contacts in UTC. In fact, as the transmissions on some frequencies can be picked up by many different time zones, they generally make reference to UTC and they could all benefit from a 24-hour watch.

Of the people belonging to the above seven groups, however, only a very small percentage use 24-hour watches. The key challenge for a broader use, as mentioned before, resides in the adoption of the 24-hour system by people that have been using the 12-hour system since they were kids. To help with the transition, some watch-makers, including Todd & Marlon, offer watches with a double-XII system.

Watches with a double-XII system are nothing more that watches with a 24-hour dial divided into two 12-hour sections. Those watches are easier to use because the way to read them is in between the two systems. People can still refer to 1-12 a.m. or 1-12 p.m., but the watch clearly differentiates day and night.

In conclusion if you are part of any of the above seven groups you might seriously consider buying and using a 24-hour watch. Be warned though! Once you get hooked on the 24-hour dial, you will never want to wear a 12-hour watch again.

THE TIME RIDER

THE TIME RIDER

ALSO BY VINCENZO CARRARA

Zordtchs (2014)

Daddy's Time
Tales and games for time together (2014)

FUMMÍ the hard working ant
basic guide to jumpstart in the work environment (2014)

FUMMÍ the hard working ant
and the great toolbox for leaders and managers (2015)

Watches-N-Time (2016)

M&A Plan for Success (2018)

Crescere con il Marketing (2018)

THE TIME RIDER

www.ingramcontent.com/pod-product-compliance
Lightning Source LLC
Chambersburg PA
CBHW070152230526
45471CB00002B/628